The Award Winning Songs

of the

COUNTRY MUSIC ASSOCIATION

A *J. Aaron Brown & Associates* Publication
in association with

HAL LEONARD
PUBLISHING
CORPORATION

Home Office: National Sales Office:
960 East Mark Street   8112 West Bluemound Road
Winona MN 55987   Milwaukee WI 53213

The Award Winning Songs
of the
COUNTRY MUSIC ASSOCIATION

The Country Music Association has been a major force behind the growth and development of country music. It was the first trade organization formed to promote a type of music. Since CMA'S founding in 1958, country music has grown from a limited, mainly regional popularity to a worldwide phenomenon. The association's membership of professionals working in the music industry has increased from 200 to more than 7,600. One of CMA's most significant achievements is its annual awards show which has been on national television since 1968, and sponsored by Kraft Foods from the beginning. Voted on by CMA members, the prestigious awards are bestowed each year to artists and songwriters who have demonstrated excellence in country music. Membership in CMA is open to those persons or organizations presently or formerly active, directly and substantially, in the field of country music.

You now hold in your hands all of the official top five songs nominated for CMA Song Of The Year from 1967 to 1983. Any country music song with original words and music is eligible based on its popularity during the year. Nominations from the CMA membership in addition to the top five songs, as tabulated from the charts of trade publications (Billboard, Cashbox, Gavin Report and Radio & Records), are voted on through balloting by the entire CMA membership. From this, the top five songs appear on the final ballot with Song Of The Year being selected and first announced on the CMA awards telecast. The entire balloting process is conducted by the international accounting firm of Deloitte Haskins And Sells.

The award for Song Of The Year goes to its songwriter or songwriters.

We hope you will enjoy all of the selections.

CONTENTS

*CMA Song Of The Year

NOMINATED SONG OF THE YEAR WRITERS AND PERFORMERS

Courtesy of CMA/
Don Putnam, Photographer

DOLLY PARTON　　　　　　　**KENNY ROGERS**

Courtesy of CMA/
Don Putnam, Photographer

EDDY ARNOLD　　　　　　**EMMYLOU HARRIS**

Courtesy of CMA/Don Putnam, Photographer

BARBARA MANDRELL

Courtesy of CMA

LORETTA LYNN

Courtesy of CMA

ALABAMA

Courtesy of CMA/Don Putnam, Photographer

JOHN ANDERSON

Courtesy of CMA/Don Putnam, Photographer

MERLE HAGGARD and WILLIE NELSON

Courtesy of CMA/
Don Putnam, Photographer

(L. to R.) LEE GREENWOOD, RONNIE MILSAP, JOHNNY CASH, ANNE MURRAY, KRIS KRISTOFFERSON, LARRY GATLIN

MEL TILLIS   LACY J. DALTON

JIMMIE DICKENS   BARBARA MANDRELL

1983 — "Little" Jimmie Dickens was inducted into Country Music Hall of Fame. Presented by Barbara Mandrell.

EDDY ARNOLD   MARTY ROBBINS

On the October 11, 1982, CMA Awards Show, Eddy Arnold presented the plaque that will be in the Country Music Hall Of Fame to Marty Robbins. The show was televised live on the CBS Network from the Grand Old Opry House.

CMA AWARD-WINNING SONGWRITERS

Courtesy of CMA/
Don Putnam, Photographer
KRIS KRISTOFFERSON
1970 — "Sunday Morning Coming Down"

Courtesy of CMA

BOBBY BRADDOCK and CURLY PUTMAN
1980 & 1981 — "He Stopped Loving Her Today"

DALLAS FRAZIER

1967 — "There Goes My Everything"

KENNY O'DELL

1973 — "Behind Closed Doors"

BOBBY RUSSELL

1968 — "Honey"

Courtesy of ASCAP **RICHARD LEIGH**
1978 — "Don't It Make My Brown Eyes Blue"

Courtesy of CMA

ROGER BOWLING   HAL BYNUM
1977 — "Lucille"

Courtesy of Nashville Songwriters Association Intl.

DON SCHLITZ
1979 — "The Gambler"

Courtesy of CMA

FREDDIE HART
1971 & 1972 — "Easy Loving"

Courtesy of CMA

JOHNNY CHRISTOPHER   **WAYNE CARSON**   **MARK JAMES**
1982 & 1983 — "Always On My Mind"

ALL THE TIME

Words and Music by WAYNE WALKER
and MEL TILLIS

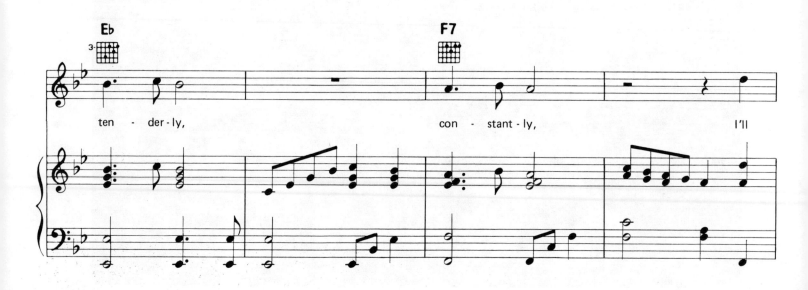

1982 & 1983 Award Winning Song
ALWAYS ON MY MIND

Words and Music by
**WAYNE THOMPSON, MARK JAMES and
JOHNNY CHRISTOPHER**

AMANDA

Words and Music by BOB McDILL

(HEY, WON'T YOU PLAY)
ANOTHER SOMEBODY DONE SOMEBODY WRONG SONG

Words and Music by LARRY BUTLER
and CHIPS MOMAN

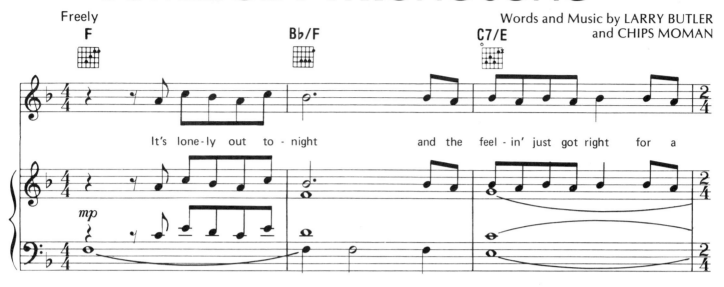

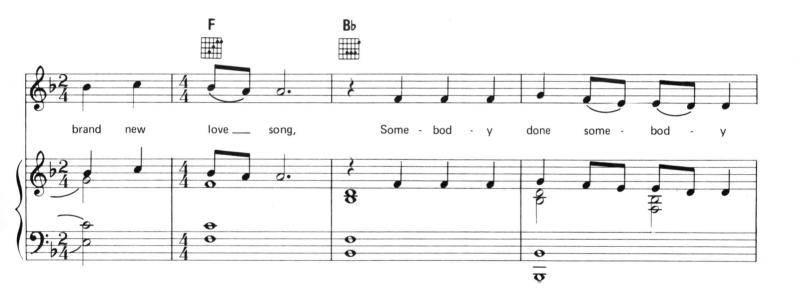

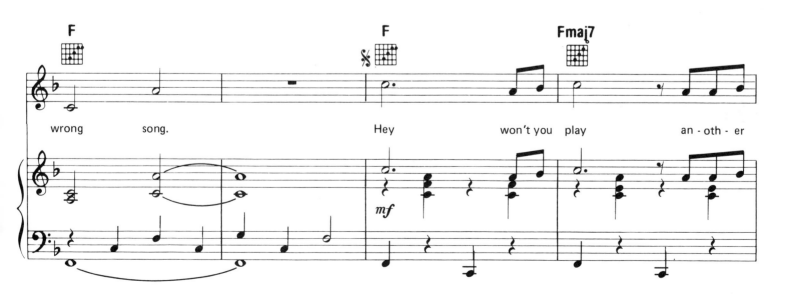

1975 *Award Winning Song*
BACK HOME AGAIN

In a relaxed 4 (♪♪♪♪ to be played ♪ ♪♪♪)

Words and Music by JOHN DENVER

There's a storm a-cross the val - ley, clouds are roll - in' in, The af - ter - noon is hea - vy on your shoul - ders There's a

CHORUS

hey it's good to be back home__ a - gain;_____

Some - times__ this old farm__ feels__ like a long- lost friend. Yes 'n'

hey it's good__ to be back home a - gain.__ There's

And oh, the time that I can lay__ this tired__ old bod - y

down and feel your fin - gers feath - er soft up on me_____

_____ The kiss - ses_____ that I live for_____ the

love that lights my way_____ the hap - pi - ness_____ that

liv - in' with you brings me_____ It's the

BEFORE THE NEXT TEARDROP FALLS

Moderately Slow

Words and Music by BEN PETERS
and VIVIAN KEITH

1973 Award Winning Song
BEHIND CLOSED DOORS

Moderately

Words & Music by KENNY O'DELL

Verse

My ba-by makes me proud, Lord, don't she make__ me proud. She nev-er makes a scene by hang-in' all o-ver me in a crowd,__ 'Cause

down, and she makes me glad I'm _____ a man; _____ Oh,

no one knows what goes on be - hind closed _____ doors.

My

be - hind closed _____ doors. _____

Verse

2. (My) baby makes me smile, Lord, don't she make me smile.
   She's never far away or too tired to say I want you.
   She's always a lady, just like a lady should be
   But when they turn out the lights, she's still a baby to me. **(Chorus)**

COAL MINER'S DAUGHTER

Words and Music by LORETTA LYNN

1969 Award Winning Song
CARROLL COUNTY ACCIDENT

Words and Music by BOB FERGUSON

1974 Award Winning Song
COUNTRY BUMPKIN

Moderate Country style

Words and Music by DON WAYNE

1. He walked in-to the bar and parked his lank-y frame up
on a tall bar stool,___
long, soft south-ern drawl, said, "I'll have me a glass of an-y-thing that's

just a short year la-ter, parked in a bed of joy-filled
tears yet death-like pain,___
to this won-drous world of man-y won-ders one more won-der

years of short hard work la-ter, in a sim-ple quiet and
peace-ful coun-try place,___
hand of time had not e-rased the rap-tured won-der from the wom-an's

COWARD OF THE COUNTY

Words and Music by ROGER BOWLING
and BILLY EDD WHEELER

Ev-'ry-one___ con-sid-ered him___ the cow-ard of___ the coun-ty,___

He'd nev-er stood_ one sin-gle time to prove the coun-ty wrong.___

His ma-ma named_ him Tom-my, the

Walk a-way from trou-ble if you can.___ It won't mean you're weak___ if you turn___ the oth-er cheek,___ I hope you're old e-nough to un-der-stand: Son, you don't have to fight to be a man."___ There's

some-one for ev-'ry one__ and Tom-my's love__ was Beck-y,__

In her arms__ he did-n't have__ to prove he was a man.

One day while he was work-in'__ the

Gat-lin boys__ came call-in', They took turns__ at Beck-y,__

As his tears fell on his dad-dy's face, he heard these words a-gain:

"Prom - ise me son, _____ not to do _____ the things I've done, Walk a -way from trou-ble if you can. _____

It won't mean you're weak _____ if you turn _____

let 'em have it all.____ When Tom-my left_ the bar - room not a

Gat - lin boy was stand-in', He said, "This one's_ for Beck - y." As he

watched the last one fall. *(Spoken) And I heard him say, "I* prom - ised you, Dad,____ not to do_

____ the things you done, I walk a - way from trou - ble when I can.___

Now please don't think I'm weak,__ I did-n't turn __ _____ the oth-er cheek,__ And Pop-pa, I sure hope you un-der-stand:___ Some - times you got - ta fight___ when you're a man." __ Ev - 'ry-one__ con - sid - ered him the cow - ard of the coun - ty._____

Slower

Guitar Tacet

DADDY SANG BASS

Words and Music by CARL PERKINS

Moderately fast

I re-mem-ber when I was a lad, times were hard and things were bad; But there's a

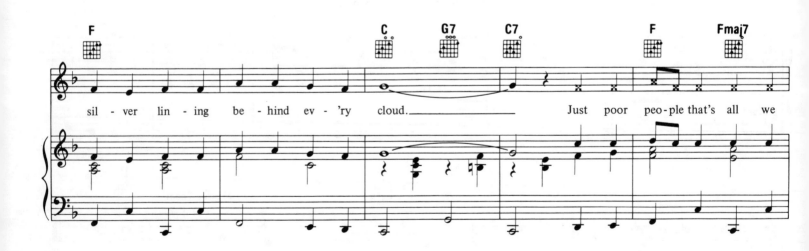

sil-ver lin-ing be-hind ev-'ry cloud._____ Just poor peo-ple that's all we

DARLING YOU KNOW I WOULDN'T LIE

Words and Music by WAYNE KEMP
and RED LANE

D-I-V-O-R-C-E

Words and Music by BOBBY BRADDOCK
& CURLY PUTMAN

THE DOOR IS ALWAYS OPEN

Words and Music by BOB McDILL
and DICKEY LEE

1978 Award Winning Song
DON'T IT MAKE MY BROWN EYES BLUE

Words and Music by RICHARD LEIGH

EASY LOVING

1971 & 1972 Award Winning Song

Words and Music by FREDDIE HART

ELVIRA

Words and Music by DALLAS FRAZIER

Verse 2. Tonight I'm gonna meet her
At the hungry house cafe
And I'm gonna give her all the love I can
She's gonna jump and holler
'Cause I saved up my last two dollar
And we're gonna search and find that preacher man
Chorus

EVERY WHICH WAY BUT LOOSE

Words and Music by STEPHEN DORFF,
MILTON BROWN and SNUFF GARRETT

THE FIGHTIN' SIDE OF ME

Words and Music by MERLE HAGGARD

1979 Award Winning Song
THE GAMBLER

Words and Music by DON SCHLITZ

GOOD OLE BOYS LIKE ME

Words and Music by BOB McDILL

When I was a kid, Uncle Remus he put me to bed,
noth-ing makes a sound in the night like the wind does,
I was in school I ran with a kid down the street,

with a pic-ture of Stone-wall Jack-son a-bove my head.
But you ain't a-fraid if you're washed in the blood like I
And I watched him burn him-self up on Bour-bon and speed.

was;
But I was smart-er than most and

Then Dad-dy came in to kiss his
The smell of Cape Jas-mine thru the

THE HAPPIEST GIRL IN THE WHOLE U.S.A.

Words and Music by
DONNA FARGO

HARPER VALLEY P.T.A.

Moderately (with a heavy beat)

Words and Music by TOM T. HALL

HEAVEN'S JUST A SIN AWAY

Words and Music by JERRY GILLESPIE

1980 & 1981 Award Winning Song
HE STOPPED LOVING HER TODAY

Words and Music by BOBBY BRADDOCK
and CURLY PUTMAN

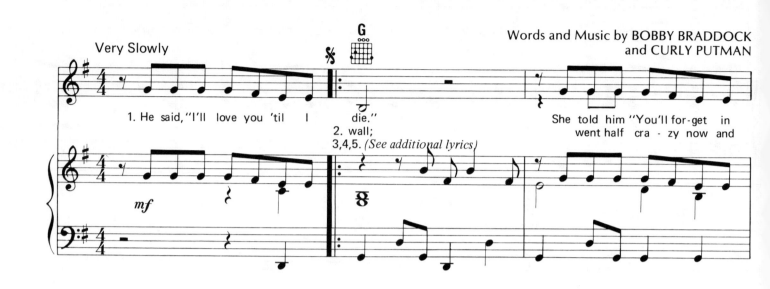

1. He said, "I'll love you 'til I die."
2. wall;
3,4,5. *(See additional lyrics)*

She told him "You'll for-get in
went half cra-zy now and

time."
then,

As the years went slow - ly by
but he still loved her through it all,

she still preyed up - on his mind.
hop - ing she'd come back a - gain.

Guitar Tacet

2. He kept her pic-ture on his
3. He kept some let-ters by his
4. I went to see him just to -

Verse 3:
He kept some letters by his bed, dated 1962.
He had underlined in red every single, "I love you".

Verse 4:
I went to see him just today, oh, but I didn't see no tears;
All dressed up to go away, first time I'd seen him smile in years.
(To Chorus:)

Verse 5: *(Spoken)*
You know, she came to see him one last time.
We all wondered if she would.
And it came running through my mind,
This time he's over her for good. (To Chorus:)

HELLO DARLIN'

Words and Music by CONWAY TWITTY

Moderate Country Waltz

Hel - lo

Dar - lin;   nice to   see you.   It's   been   a   long   time;   you're just as
Dar - lin;   let me   kiss you,   just   been   for   old   times   sake.   Let me

love - ly   as   you   used   to   be.   How's your
hold you   in my   arms   one more   time.   Thank you

1968 *Award Winning Song*
HONEY

Words and Music by
BOBBY RUSSELL

Moderately

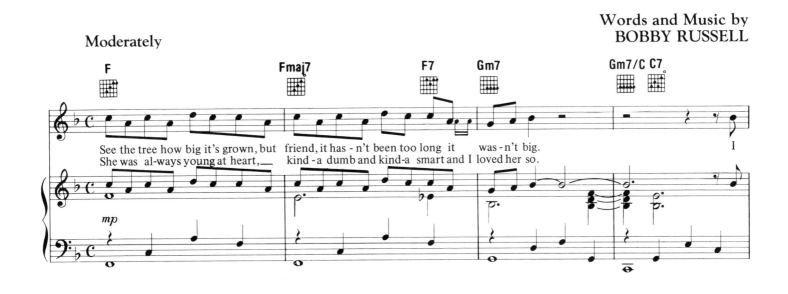

See the tree how big it's grown, but friend, it has-n't been too long it was-n't big. I
She was al-ways young at heart,___ kind-a dumb and kind-a smart and I loved her so.

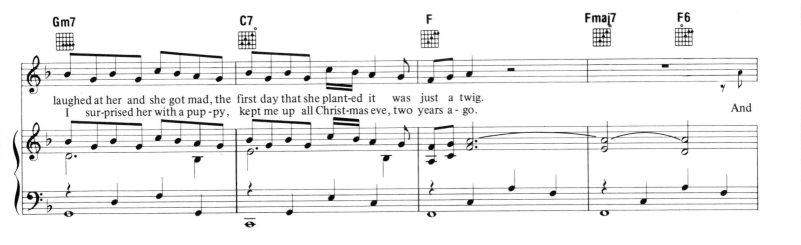

laughed at her and she got mad, the first day that she plant-ed it was just a twig. And
I sur-prised her with a pup-py, kept me up all Christ-mas eve, two years a-go.

Then the first snow came and she ran out to brush the snow a-way so it would-n't die, Came
it would sure em-bar-rass her when I came home from work-ing late 'cause I would know That

I BELIEVE IN YOU

Words and Music by
ROGER COOK and SAM HOGIN

Moderately

I don't be-lieve in su-per-stars, or-gan-ic food and for-eign cars, I
don't be-lieve that heav-en waits for on-ly those who con-gre-gate, I
don't be-lieve vir-gin-i-ty is as com-mon as it used to be, in

don't be-lieve the price of gold, the cer-tain-ty of grow-ing old, that
like to think of God as love, He's down be-low, He's up a-bove, He's
work-ing days and sleep-ing nights that black is black and white is white, that

I WAS COUNTRY
WHEN COUNTRY WASN'T COOL

Words and Music by KYE FLEMING
and DENNIS MORGAN

Verse 2:
I remember circling the drive-in,
Pulling up, and turning down George Jones.
I remember when no one was looking,
I was putting peanuts in my coke.
I took a lot of kidding, 'cause I never did fit in;
Now look at everybody trying to be what I was then;
I was country, when country wasn't cool.

Verse 3:
They called us country bumpkins for sticking to our roots;
I'm just glad we're in a country where we're all free to choose;
I was country, when country wasn't cool.

I'LL GET OVER YOU

Words and Music by RICHARD LEIGH

(I'M A)
STAND BY MY WOMAN MAN

Moderate (Steady Beat)

Words and Music by KENT ROBBINS

2. When she's down, she knows I'll be beside her,
   'Cause I'm not just her lover, I'm her friend.
   Our love keeps getting better and I'll gladly spend forever
   Standing by the woman who stands by her man.
   I'm a. . . . .

I'M JUST AN OLD CHUNK OF COAL
(BUT I'M GONNA BE A DIAMOND SOMEDAY)

With a Driving Beat

Words and Music by BILLY JOE SHAVER

I'M GONNA HIRE A WINO TO
DECORATE OUR HOME

Words and Music by
DeWAYNE BLACKWELL

I came crawl-in' home___ last night___ like man-y nights be-fore___

I final-ly made it to my feet___ as she o-pened up___ the door___ And she said

you're not gon-na do___ this an - y more

She said I'm___ Gon - na Hire A

Wi - no To Dec -'rate___ Our Home___ So you'll feel more at ease here___ and

bring those Fri - day pay-checks and I'll cash -'em all___ right here___ 'n' I'll keep on tap for all your friends___ their

rip out all the car - pet put saw-dust on___ the floor___ serve hard boiled eggs 'n' pret - zels___ and

131

I'M NOT LISA

Words and Music by JESSI COLTER

Moderately Slow

I.O.U.

Words and Music by
AUSTIN ROBERTS & KERRY CHATER

Moderately Slow Ballad

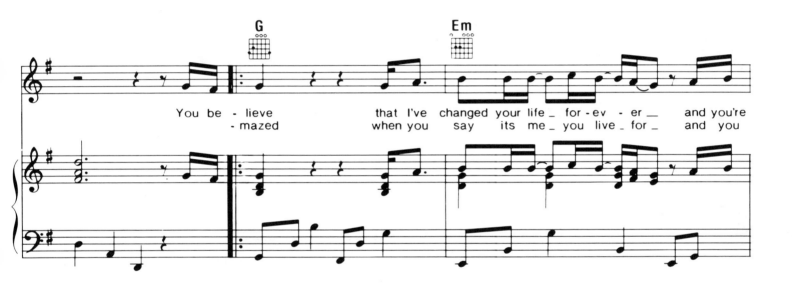

You be - lieve that I've changed your life _ for - ev - er _ and you're
- mazed when you say its me _ you live _ for _ and you

nev - er gon - na find _ an - oth - er some - bod - y like me. _ And you
know that when _ I'm hold - ing, you you're right where you be - long. _ And my

IF WE MAKE IT THROUGH DECEMBER

Words and Music by MERLE HAGGARD

Steadily

If we make it through De - cem - ber _____ ev - 'ry - thing's gon - na be al - right, I know; _____ It's the cold -

IF YOU LOVE ME
(LET ME KNOW)

Words and Music by JOHN ROSTILL

You came when I was hap - py; in your sun - shine.

I grew to love you more___ each pass - ing day.___

Be - fore too long___ I built___ my world___ a - round you.

145

Any time ___ I turn a - round ___ to find ___ you there. ___

It's this and so much more ___ that makes ___ me love you. ___

What else can ___ I do ___ to make you see? ___

You know you have ___ what - ev - er's mine ___ to give you,

IF YOU'RE GONNA DO ME WRONG

(DO IT RIGHT)

Words and Music by VERN GOSDIN
and MAX BARNES

150

IT TURNS ME INSIDE OUT

Words and Music by JAN CRUTCHFIELD

In a way I'm glad it's o-ver, e-ven though it's gon-na hurt me once you're gone.
way I guess it's bet-ter, e-ven though there's noth-in' good a-bout good-bye.

But I can learn to live with-out you, give me time and I can make it on my
But I know I could-n't hold you, now you've found new wings and you need room to

own.
fly.

Lov-in' you to me came eas-y, now los-in' you will change my life no
It's for sure I'm gon-na miss you, but I guess that's what good-bye is all a-

IN AMERICA

Words and Music by CHARLIE DANIELS,
TOM CRAIN, "TAZ" DiGREGORIO, FRED EDWARDS,
CHARLIE HAYWARD and JIM MARSHALL

never did think that it ever would hap-pen a-gain.

From the

IT WAS ALMOST LIKE A SONG

Words and Music by ARCHIE JORDAN
and HAL DAVID

Once in ev-'ry life, / You were in my arms,

some-one comes a- / just where you be-

long, / we were so in love.

and you came to me.

IT'S NOT LOVE
(BUT IT'S NOT BAD)

Words and Music by GLENN MARTIN
and HANK COCHRAN

IT'S SUCH A PRETTY WORLD TODAY

Words and Music by DALE NOE

KISS AN ANGEL GOOD MORNIN'

Moderately

By BEN PETERS

1. When
2. (Well)

ev - er I chance to meet____ some old friends____ on the____ street.
peo - ple may try to guess____ the se - cret of hap - pi - ness,____

They won - der how does a man____ get to be this way.
But some of them nev - er learn,____ it's a sim - ple thing.

let her know you think a - bout her when you're gone ___

Kiss An An - gel Good - Morn - in' and love her like the dev - il when you

get back home ___

2. Well,

get back home. ___

get back home ___

THE LAST GAME OF THE SEASON
(THE BLIND MAN IN THE BLEACHERS)

Words and Music by STERLING WHIPPLE

Moderate Country 2

(Spoken:) He's just the blind man in the bleach-ers to the lo - cal home town fans, And he sits be-neath the speak - ers, way back in the stands, And he

LITTLE GREEN APPLES

Words and Music by
BOBBY RUSSELL

1977 *Award Winning Song*
LUCILLE

Words and Music by ROGER BOWLING
and HAL BYNUM

LUCKENBACH, TEXAS
(Back To The Basics Of Love)

Words and Music by BOBBY EMMONS
and CHIPS MOMAN

(in tempo)

back to the ba-sics of love. Let's go to Luck-en-bach, Tex - as, with

Way-lon and Wil - lie and the boys. This suc-

ces-ful life we're liv-in' got us feud-in' like the Hat-fields and_ Mc - Coys.

Be - tween_ Hank Wil - liam's pain songs and New-ber-ry's train songs and

MAMMAS DON'T LET YOUR BABIES GROW UP TO BE COWBOYS

Country Waltz

Words and Music by ED BRUCE
and PATSY BRUCE

THE MOST BEAUTIFUL GIRL

Words and Music by NORRIS WILSON,
BILLY SHERRILL and RAY BOURKE

Hey, did you hap-pen to see___ the most beau-ti-ful girl___ in the world?

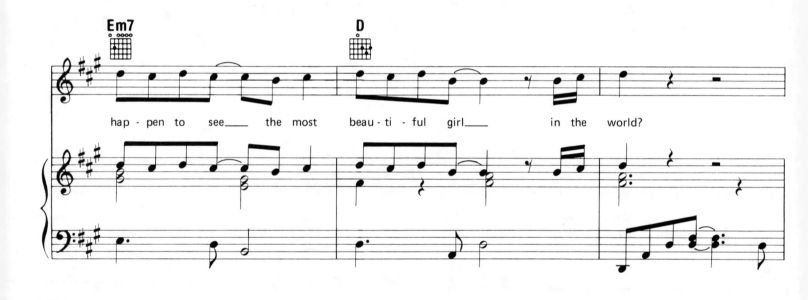

And if you did,___ was___ she cry-ing,

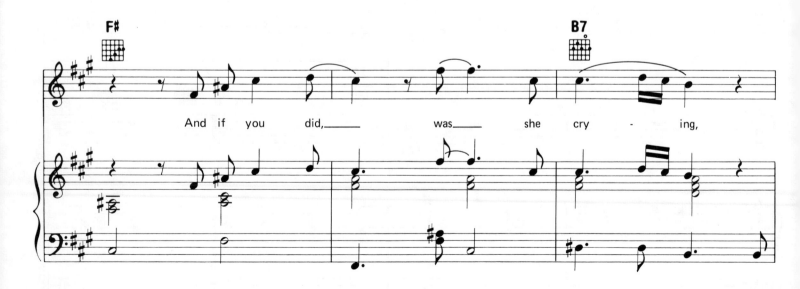

MY ELUSIVE DREAMS

Words and Music by CURLY PUTMAN
and BILLY SHERRILL

1. You fol-lowed me ___ to Tex-as, You fol-lowed me ___ to U-tah,

2,3 (See additional lyrics)

We did-n't find it there so we moved on. ___ You

fol-lowed me ___ to Al-a-bam', Things looked good in Bir-ming-ham,

2. You had my child in Memphis, I heard of work in Nashville,
   We didn't find it there so we moved on.
   To a small farm in Nebraska to a gold mine in Alaska,
   We didn't find it there so we moved on. (Chorus)

3. And now we've left Alaska because there was no gold mine,
   But this time only two of us move on.
   Now all we have is each other and a little memory to cling to,
   And still you won't let me go on alone. (Chorus)

MY WOMAN, MY WOMAN, MY WIFE

Words and Music by MARTY ROBBINS

ODE TO BILLY JOE

Words & Music by BOBBIE GENTRY

It was the third of June,— an-oth-er

sleep - y, dust - y, del - ta day,_____ I was

out___ chop-pin' cot - ton and my broth - er was bail - in' hay:_____

Bil - ly Joe Mc Al - lis - ter jumped off the Tal - la - hat - chee Bridge."

2. Papa said to Mama, as he passed around the black-eyed peas,
   "Well, Billy Joe never had a lick o' sense, pass the biscuits please,
   There's five more acres in the lower forty I've got to plow,"
   And Mama said it was a shame about Billy Joe anyhow.
   Seems like nothin' ever comes to no good up on Choctaw Ridge,
   And now Billy Joe McAllister's jumped off the Tallahatchee Bridge.

3. Brother said he recollected when he and Tom and Billy Joe,
   Put a frog down my back at the Carroll County picture show,
   And wasn't I talkin' to him after church last Sunday night,
   I'll have another piece of apple pie, you know, it don't seem right.
   I saw him at the sawmill yesterday on Choctaw Ridge,
   And now you tell me Billy Joe's jumped off the Tallahatchee Bridge.

4. Mama said to me, "Child what's happened to your appetite?
   I been cookin' all mornin' and you haven't touched a single bite,
   That nice young preacher Brother Taylor dropped by today,
   Said he'd be pleased to have dinner on Sunday, Oh, by the way,
   He said he saw a girl that looked a lot like you up on Choctaw Ridge
   And she an' Billy Joe was throwin' somethin' off the Tallahatchee Bridge."

5. A year has come and gone since we heard the news 'bout Billy Joe,
   Brother married Becky Thompson, they bought a store in Tupelo,
   There was a virus goin' 'round, Papa caught it and he died last spring,
   And now Mama doesn't seem to want to do much of anything.
   And me I spend a lot of time pickin' flowers up on Choctaw Ridge,
   And drop them into the muddy water off the Tallahatchee Bridge.

OKIE FROM MUSKOGEE

Words and Music by MERLE HAGGARD
and ROY EDWARD BURRIS

Moderately fast

1. We don't smoke mar - i - jua - na in Mus - ko - gee,
2. We don't make a par - ty out of lov - ing,
boots are still in style if a man needs foot - wear,

And we don't take our trips on L. S.
But we like hold - ing hands and pitch - ing
Beads and Ro - man san - dals won't be

place where e - ven squares can have a ball.

We still wave Ol' Glo - ry down at the Court House, White light - ning's still the big - gest thrill of all.

3. Leath - er

OLD DOGS, CHILDREN AND WATERMELON WINE

Words and Music by
TOM T. HALL

Moderato

3. Ever had a drink of watermelon wine? He asked.
   He told me all about it though I didn't answer back.
   Ain't but three things in this world that's worth a solitary dime,
   But OLD DOGS - CHILDREN AND WATERMELON WINE.

4. He said women think about theyselves when menfolk ain't around,
   And friends are hard to find when they discover that you down.
   He said I tried it all when I was young and in my natural prime;
   Now it's OLD DOGS - CHILDREN AND WATERMELON WINE.

5. Old dogs care about you even when you make mistakes.
   God bless little children while they're still too young to hate.
   When he moved away, I found my pen and copied down that line
   'Bout old dogs and children and watermelon wine.

6. I had to catch a plane up to Atlanta that next day,
   As I left for my room I saw him pickin' up my change.
   That night I dreamed in peaceful sleep of shady summertime
   Of old dogs and children and watermelon wine.

PUT YOUR HAND IN THE HAND

By GENE MacLELLAN

With a beat

Chorus

Put Your Hand In The Hand of the Man who stilled __ the wa -

Put Your Hand In The Hand of the

Man who calmed ___ the sea; _____ Take a

RAINY DAY WOMAN

Words and Music by WAYLON JENNINGS

1976 Award Winning Song
RHINESTONE COWBOY

Words and Music by LARRY WEISS

SATIN SHEETS

Words and Music by JOHN E. VOLINKATY

Sat - in sheets to lie on, Sat - in pil - lows to cry on, still, I'm not hap - py don't you see. Big long Cad - il - lacs, tail - or mades up-

Bb

can't hold me tight ___ like he does _____ on a long, long night. _

F **C7** **1,2 F**

You know ___ you did-n't keep me sat - is - fied. _____
die. _____

3 F

D.S. al Coda

eyes _____

CODA

ADDITIONAL VERSES

2. We've been through thick and thin together
   Braved the fair and stormy weather
   We've had all the hard times, you and I.
   And now that I'm a big success
   You called today and you confessed
   And told me things that made me want to die.

3. You told me there's another woman
   Who can give more than I can,
   And I've given ev'rything that cash will buy.
   You can't buy me a peaceful night
   With loving arms around me tight
   And you're too busy to notice the hurt in my eyes.

SHE BELIEVES IN ME

Words & Music by STEVE GIB[...]

Slowly with movement

While she lays sleep - ing, I stay out late at night __ and play my

songs, ____ And some - times all the nights __ can be so long, And it's

good when I fin - 'ly make it home all a - lone. While she lays

SHE'S ALL I GOT

Words and Music by JERRY WILLIAMS JR.
and GARY BONDS

16TH AVENUE

Words and Music by THOM SCHUYLER

SKIP A ROPE

Words and Music by JACK MORAN
and GLENN D. TUBB

238

STAND BY YOUR MAN

Words and Music by TAMMY WYNETTE and
BILLY SHERRILL

SOUTHERN NIGHTS

Words and Music by ALLEN TOUSSAINT

THE STREAK

Words and Music by RAY STEVENS

"Hello, everyone, this is your action news reporter with all the news that is news across the nation. On the scene at the super market; there seems to have been some disturbance here. Pardon me, sir, did you see what happened? 'Yeh, I did. I was standing over there by the tomatoes, and here he come. Runnin' through the pole beans, through the fruits and vegetables, naked as a jay-bird. And I hollered over at Ethel; I said, "Don't look, Ethel!" It was too late; she'd already been incensed."

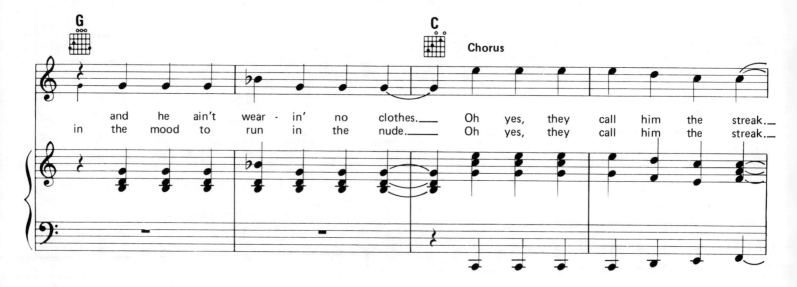

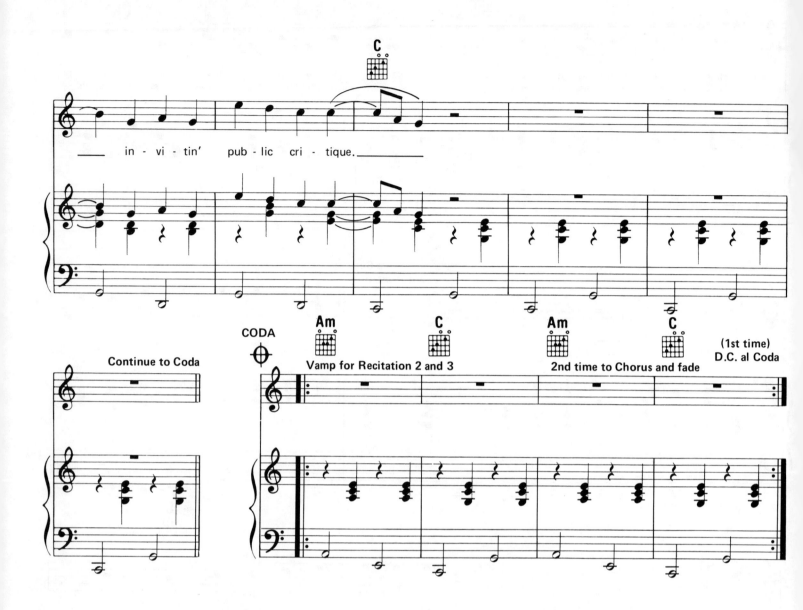

Continue to Coda

CODA

Vamp for Recitation 2 and 3

2nd time to Chorus and fade

(1st time)
D.C. al Coda

in - vi - tin' pub - lic cri - tique.

Recitation 2

"This is your action news reporter once again, and we're here at the gas station. Pardon me, sir, did you see what happened? 'Yeh, I did. I was just in here gettin' my tires checked, and he just appeared out of the traffic. Come streakin' around the grease rack there, didn't have nothin' on but a smile. I looked in there and Ethel was gettin' her a cold drink. I hollered, "Don't look, Ethel!" It was too late. She'd already been mooned. Flashed her right there in front of the shock absorbers."

Recitation 3

"Once again, your action news reporter in the booth at the gym covering the disturbance at the basketball playoffs. Pardon me, sir, did you see what happened? 'Yeh, I did. Half-time, I was just going down there to get Ethel a snow-cone. Here he come, right out of the cheap seats, dribblin', right down the middle of the court. Didn't have nothin' on but his P.F.'s. Made a hook shot and got out through the concession stand. I hollered at Ethel, I said, "Don't look, Ethel!" It was too late. She'd already got a free shot. Grandstanded . . . right there in front of the home team."

(Repeat Chorus and recite over:) *"Here he comes. Look who's that with him? Ethel! Is that you, Ethel? What do you think you're doing? You get your clothes on! Ethel, where you going? Ethel, you shameless hussy! Say it isn't so, Ethel. Ethel . . . .!* **(Fade Chorus)**

1970 Award Winning Song

SUNDAY MORNING COMIN' DOWN

Moderate rock beat

Words & Music by KRIS KRISTOFFERSON

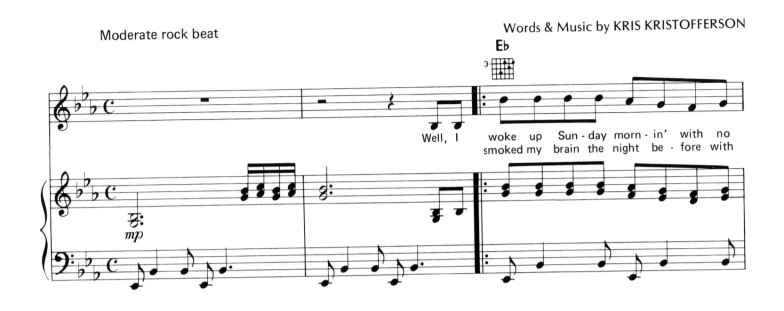

Well, I woke up Sun-day morn-in' with no
smoked my brain the night be-fore with

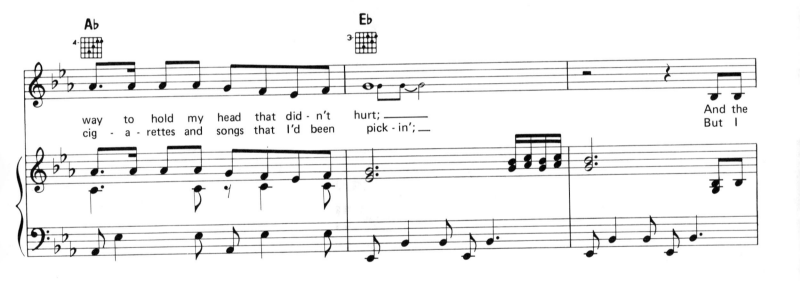

way to hold my head that did-n't hurt; ___
cig-a-rettes and songs that I'd been pick-in'; ___

And the
But I

beer I had for break-fast was-n't bad, so I had one more for des-sert; ___
lit my first and watched a small kid cuss-in' at a can that he was kick-in'; ___

Then I fum-bled through my clos-et for my clothes and found my clean-est___ dir-ty
Then I crossed the emp-ty street and caught the Sun-day smell of some-one___ fry-in'

shirt; _____
chick-en; ___

And I shaved my face, and combed my hair, and
And it

stum-bled down the stair to meet the day._____

I'd took me back to some-thin' that I'd

lost some-how some-where a-long the way.

On the Sun-day morn-in'

In the park I saw a daddy with a laughing little girl that he was swingin';
And I stopped beside a Sunday School and listened to the song that they were singin';
Then I headed back for home, and somewhere far away a lonely bell was ringin';
And it echoed thru the canyon like the disappearing dreams of yesterday.

SWINGIN'

Words and Music by JOHN DAVID ANDERSON
and LIONEL A. DELMORE

With a strong beat

1. There's ____ a lit-tle girl in our neigh-bor-hood. Her
2.3. (See additional lyrics)

name is Char-lotte John-son, and she's real-ly look-ing good. I had to go and see her, so I

called her on the phone. I walked o-ver to her house,— and this was go-in' on: 2. Her

Verse 2.

Her brother was on the sofa
Eatin' chocolate pie.
Her mama was in the kitchen
Cuttin' chicken up to fry.
Her daddy was in the backyard
Rollin' up a garden hose.
I was on the porch with Charlotte
Feelin' love down to my toes,
And we was swingin'. *(To Chorus:)*

Verse 3.

Now Charlotte, she's a darlin';
She's the apple of my eye.
When I'm on the swing with her
It makes me almost high.
And Charlotte is my lover.
And she has been since the spring.
I just can't believe it started
On her front porch in the swing. *(To Chorus:)*

TAKE THIS JOB AND SHOVE IT

Words and Music by DAVID ALLEN COE

Take this job ___ and shove it! I ain't work-in' here no more. ___ My wom-an done left and took all the rea-sons I was work-in' for. ___ You bet-ter not try to stand in my way; ___ 'cause I'm

I've seen a lot of good___ folk die___ that had a lot of bills to pay.___
One of these days I'm gon-na blow my top.___ That suck-er, he's gon-na pay.___

I'd give the shirt right off___ of my back if I had the guts___ to say:___
Lord, I can't wait to see___ their fac-es when I get the nerve___ to say:___

more. Take this job and

shove it!

TALKIN' IN YOUR SLEEP

Words and Music by ROGER COOK
and BOBBY WOODS

1967 Award Winning Song
THERE GOES MY EVERYTHING

Words and Music by DALLAS FRAZIER

TILL I CAN MAKE IT ON MY OWN

Words and Music by TAMMY WYNETTE,
BILLY SHERRILL and GEORGE RICHEY

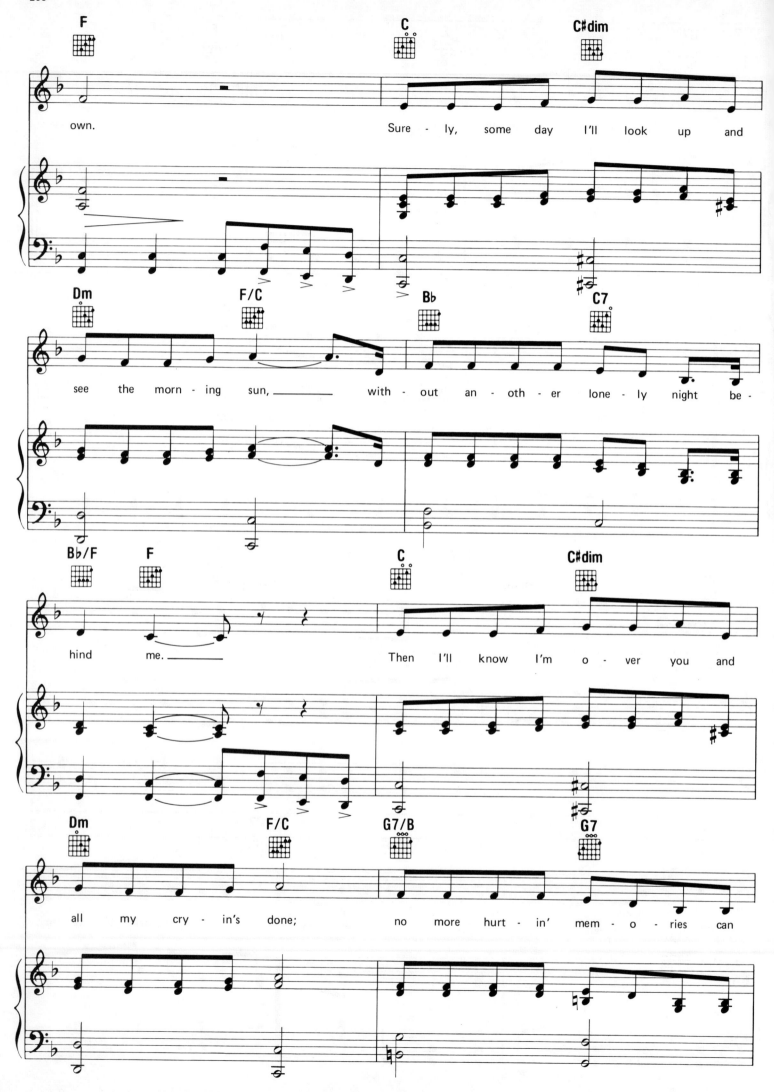

Verse 5: But 'til then, Lord, you know I'm gonna need a friend.
'Til I get used to losing you, let me keep on using you,
'Til I can make it on my own.

TO GET TO YOU

Words and Music by JEAN CHAPEL

Moderate Country Waltz

I would

walk out on my friends do, to get to you.
last thing I do, I'll get to you. If I
Just be-

lose them all for your love, I'll do that too. ___
Cause I know just how much you want me to. ___

WHEN THE GRASS GROWS OVER ME

Words and Music by DON CHAPEL

Thoughtfully

mf

G

C/G G

Csus C

When you left I thought that I would soon get ov - er you;____
When my eyes are closed they keep on see - ing you;____

D7

G

____ E - ven told my - self that I would find some - bod - y, too____
Ev - 'ry min - ute I'm a - live I'm hurt - ing through and through.____

C/G G

____ Time and tears have come and gone but not your
And as long as I live I know I

273

WHEN YOU'RE HOT, YOU'RE HOT

Bright Tempo

Words and Music by JERRY REED HUBBARD

(Spoken) (1)   Well now,

me and Homer Jones and Big John Talley had a big crap game goin' back in the alley; and
time I rolled 'em dice I'd win, and I would just get ready to roll 'em a-gain, when I
took us into court I couldn't be-lieve my eyes___ The judge was a fishin' buddy that I recognised. I said, "Hey

I kept rollin' them sevens and winnin' all them pots. My
heard something behind me and I turned around and there was a big ole cop. He said,
Judge, old buddy old pal. I'll pay you that hundred I owe you if you get me out of this spot." So he

THE YEAR THAT CLAYTON DELANEY DIED

Words and Music by TOM T. HALL

I re-mem-ber the year ___ that Clay-ton De-lan-ey
Clay-ton was the best ___ gui-tar pick-er in our
Dad-dy said he drank a lot, but I could nev-er un-der

died; They said for the last two ___
town; I thought he was a he-ro, and I
stand; I knew he used to pick up in O-

weeks that he suf-fered and cried.
used to fol-low Clay-ton a-round.
hi - o with a five - piece band.

It
I

WHY ME LORD?

Words and Music by KRIS KRISTOFFERSON

YOU DECORATED MY LIFE

Words and Music by BOB MORRISON
and DEBBIE HUPP

YOU'RE THE REASON GOD MADE OKLAHOMA

Words and Music by
SANDY PINKARD and LARRY COLLINS

2. Here the city lights outshine the moon
   I was just now thinking of you
   Sometimes when the wind blows you can see the mountains
   And all the way to Malibu
   Everyone's a star here in L.A. County
   You ought to see the things that they do.
   All the cowboys down on the Sunset Strip
   Wish they could be like you.
   The Santa Monica Freeway
   Sometimes makes a country girl blue

   (BRIDGE)

3. I worked ten hours on a John Deere tractor,
   Just thinkin of you all day....
   I've got a calico cat and a two
   room flat, on a
   street in West L.A.

SONGWRITERS OF NOMINATED CMA SONGS

(* CMA Song Of The Year)

John Anderson
Swingin'
Max D. Barnes
If You're Gonna Do Me Wrong
   (Do It Right)
DeWayne Blackwell
I'm Gonna Hire A Wino To
   Decorate Our Home
Gary Bond
She's All I've Got
Rory Bourke
The Most Beautiful Girl
Roger Bowling
Coward Of The County
Lucille *1977
Bobby Braddock
D-I-V-O-R-C-E
He Stopped Loving Her Today
   *1980, 1981
Milton Brown
Every Which Way But Loose
Ed Bruce
Mammas, Don't Let Your Babies
   Grow Up To Be Cowboys
Patsy Bruce
Mammas, Don't Let Your Babies
   Grow Up To Be Cowboys
Roy Edward Burris
Okie From Muskogee
Larry Butler
(Hey Won't You Play)
   Another Somebody Done
   Somebody Wrong Song
Hal Bynum
Lucille *1977
Don Chapel
When The Grass Grows Over Me
Jean Chapel
To Get To You
Kerry Chater
I.O.U.
Johnny Christopher
Always On My Mind *1982, 1983
Hank Cochran
It's Not Love (But It Ain't Bad)
David Allen Coe
Take This Job And Shove It
Larry Collins
You're The Reason God
   Made Oklahoma
Jessi Colter
I'm Not Lisa
Roger Cook
I Believe In You
Talkin' In Your Sleep
Tom Crain
In America
Jan Crutchfield
It Turns Me Inside Out
Charlie Daniels
In America
Hal David
It Was Almost Like A Song
Lionel Delmore
Swingin'
John Denver
Back Home Again *1975
"Taz" DiGregorio
In America
Stephen Dorff
Every Which Way But Loose
Fred Edwards
In America
Bobby Emmons
Luckenbach, Texas
Donna Fargo
The Happiest Girl In The
   Whole U.S.A.
Bob Ferguson
Carroll County Accident *1969

Kye Fleming
I Was Country When Country
   Wasn't Cool
Dallas Frazier
Elvira
There Goes My Everything *1967
Snuff Garrett
Every Which Way But Loose
Bobbie Gentry
Ode To Billie Joe
Steve Gibb
She Believes In Me
Jerry Gillespie
Heaven's Just A Sin Away
Vern Gosdin
If You're Gonna Do Me Wrong
   (Do It Right)
Merle Haggard
The Fightin' Side Of Me
If We Make It Through December
Okie From Muskogee
Tom T. Hall
Harper Valley P.T.A.
Old Dogs, Children And
   Watermelon Wine
The Year That Clayton Delaney Died
Freddie Hart
Easy Loving *1971, 1972
Charlie Hayward
In America
Sam Hogin
I Believe In You
Debbie Hupp
You Decorated My Life
Mark James
Always On My Mind *1982, 1983
Waylon Jennings
Rainy Day Woman
Archie Jordan
It Was Almost Like A Song
Vivian Keith
Before The Next Teardrop Falls
Wayne Kemp
Darling You Know I Wouldn't Lie
Kris Kristofferson
Sunday Morning Comin'
   Down *1970
Why Me Lord?
Red Lane
Darling You Know I Wouldn't Lie
Dickey Lee
The Door Is Always Open
Richard Leigh
Don't It Make My Brown Eyes
   Blue *1978
I'll Get Over You
Loretta Lynn
Coal Miner's Daughter
Gene MacLellan
Put Your Hand In The Hand
Jim Marshall
In America
Glenn Martin
It's Not Love (But It Ain't Bad)
Bob McDill
Amanda
The Door Is Always Open
Good Ole Boys Like Me
Chips Moman
(Hey Won't You Play)
   Another Somebody Done
   Somebody Wrong Song
Luckenbach, Texas
Jack Moran
Skip A Rope
Dennis Morgan
I Was Country When Country
   Wasn't Cool
Bob Morrison
You Decorated My Life
Dale Noe
It's Such A Pretty World Today

Kenny O'Dell
Behind Closed Doors *1973
Carl Perkins
Daddy Sang Bass
Ben Peters
Before The Next Teardrop Falls
Kiss An Angel Good Morning
Sandy Pinkard
You're The Reason God
   Made Oklahoma
Curly Putman
D-I-V-O-R-C-E
He Stopped Loving Her Today
   *1980, 1981
My Elusive Dreams
Jerry Reed
When You're Hot, You're Hot
George Richey
Till I Can Make It On My Own
Kent Robbins
(I'm A) Stand By Your
   Woman Man
Marty Robbins
My Woman, My Woman, My Wife
Austin Roberts
I.O.U.
John Rostill
If You Love Me (Let Me Know)
Bobby Russell
Honey *1968
Little Green Apples
Don Schlitz
The Gambler *1979
Thomas Schuyler
16th Avenue
Billy Joe Shaver
I'm Just An Old Chunk Of Coal
Billy Sherrill
The Most Beautiful Girl
My Elusive Dreams
Stand By Your Man
Till I Can Make It On My Own
Ray Stevens
The Streak
Wayne Thompson (Wayne Carson)
Always On My Mind *1982, 1983
Mel Tillis
All The Time
Allen Toussaint
Southern Nights
Glenn Tubb
Skip A Rope
Conway Twitty
Hello Darlin'
John Volinkaty
Satin Sheets
Wayne Walker
All The Time
Don Wayne
Country Bumpkin *1974
Larry Weiss
Rhinestone Cowboy *1976
Billy Edd Wheeler
Coward Of The County
Sterling Whipple
The Last Game Of The Season
   (The Blind Man In The Bleachers)
Jerry Williams, Jr.
She's All I've Got
Norro Wilson
The Most Beautiful Girl
Bobby Woods
Talkin' In Your Sleep
Tammy Wynette
Stand By Your Man
Till I Can Make It On My Own